Extraordinary Lives

HORATIO NELSON

Jane Bingham

WAYLAND

First published in 2010 by Wayland

Wayland
338 Euston Road
London NW1 3BH

Wayland Australia
Level 17/207 Kent Street
Sydney NSW 2000

Editor: Katie Powell
Designer: Phipps Design
Picture Researcher: Shelley Noronha

British Library Cataloguing in Publication Data

Bingham, Jane.
   Horatio Nelson. – (Extraordinary lives)
   1. Nelson, Horatio Nelson, Viscount, 1758-1805–Juvenile literature.
   2. Admirals–Great Britain–Biography–Juvenile literature.
   3. Great Britain–History, Naval–18th century–Juvenile literature.
   I. Title II. Series
   359.3'31'092-dc22

ISBN: 978 0 7502 6048 0

Picture acknowledgements: Cover © National Maritime Museum, p4 © The Art Archive /
Musée du Château de Versailles / Gianni Dagli Orti, p5 © Wayland, p6 © Private Collection /
Ken Welsh / The Bridgeman Art Library , p7 © National Maritime Museum, Greenwich,
London, p8 © Private Collection / Look and Learn/ The Bridgeman Art Library, p9 © The Print
Collector / HIP /TopFoto, p10 © CORBIS, p11 © National Maritime Museum, Greenwich,
London, p12 © National Maritime Museum, Greenwich, London, p13 © Joseph Sohm; Visions
of America /CORBIS, p14 © TopFoto, p15 © The Art Archive / Marc Charmet, p16 © The Art
Archive / Harper Collins Publishers, p17 © The Art Archive / Gunshots, p18 © Mary Evans
Picture Library, p19 © iStock, p20 © Lady Hamilton (c.1765–1815) (oil on canvas) by Schmidt,
Johann Heinrich (1749–1829) Great Cabin, H.M.S. Victory / The Bridgeman Art Library, p 21
© National Maritime Museum, Greenwich, London, p22 © Wayland, p23 © HMS *Victory* by
Howat, Andrew (20th Century) Private Collection / © Look and Learn/ The Bridgeman Art
Library, p24 © Mary Evans Picture Library, p25 © Wayland (NMM), p26 © National Maritime
Museum, Greenwich, London, p27 © iStock.

Printed in China

Wayland is a division of Hachette Children's Books, an Hachette UK company.
www.hachette.co.uk

Contents

Words that appear in **bold** can be found in the glossary.

Horatio Nelson –
an extraordinary naval hero

Nelson paced the deck of HMS *Victory* as his crew prepared for battle. Just the sight of him, with his medals glinting, filled his men with courage. With **Admiral** Nelson as their leader, they were confident they would win a great victory.

Admiral Nelson's uniform was covered with the many medals he had won.

A brave leader

Nelson's crew were preparing for the Battle of Trafalgar, a fight between the British and the French. The French were led by Napoleon Bonaparte, who had threatened to invade Britain. Nelson needed to win to keep his country safe.

A DRAMATIC LIFE

Nelson died at the age of 39, but he had many achievements in his short life. He won three very important battles: the Battle of Cape St. Vincent, the Battle of the Nile and the Battle of Trafalgar. He was also wounded several times, losing his right arm and the sight in one eye.

Just before the fighting began, one of Nelson's captains tried to give him some advice. The captain was afraid that Nelson would be an easy target for the enemy, and he asked him to cover up his medals. Nelson bravely refused to change his clothes. He was proud of his medals, which showed that he had won many victories at sea. He also wanted his men to be able to see him and feel reassured that he was in charge.

A great victory

During the battle, Nelson was spotted by an enemy gunman and shot through the back. It was a fatal wound and he died a few hours later. Before he died, Nelson heard the news that the British had won. His last words were, 'Thank God I have done my duty'.

This map shows the key places associated with Nelson.

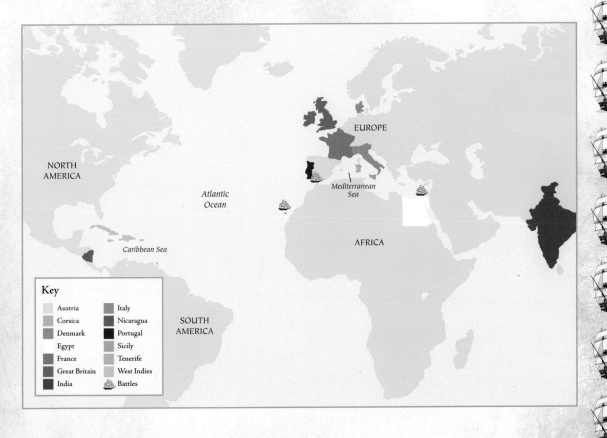

NORTH AMERICA

EUROPE

Atlantic Ocean

Mediterranean Sea

AFRICA

Caribbean Sea

SOUTH AMERICA

Key

Austria
Corsica
Denmark
Egypt
France
Great Britain
India
Italy
Nicaragua
Portugal
Sicily
Tenerife
West Indies
Battles

Young Nelson

Horatio Nelson was born on 29 September 1758. His father was the **vicar** at Burnham Thorpe, a small village in Norfolk, close to the sea. Nelson was the third of five boys in a family of eight children.

A **country childhood**

Nelson had a quiet country childhood. His father was gentle but strict, and the family spent a lot of time in church. Nelson's mother died when he was only nine, but by that time he was away at school.

The Nelson family home was pulled down in 1802. In this painting, the artist has imagined a scene from Nelson's childhood.

Nelson attended two boarding schools, where he gained a name for being a daredevil. One night he sneaked out of school and stole some pears from the headmaster's garden. Then he shared the fruit with his friends!

Dreams of the sea

When he was home at Burnham Thorpe, Nelson liked to visit the local fishermen. They fished from barges or small boats, but Nelson dreamed of sailing in much larger ships.

By the time he was 12 years old, Nelson had a plan. He had an uncle, Captain Maurice Suckling, who was an officer in the British **navy**. Nelson asked his father if he could join his uncle's ship, and train to be a sailor. His father was surprised, but he recognised that nothing would stop his son from going to sea.

A TOUGH CHOICE

Nelson was a small, skinny boy, who didn't seem strong enough to be a sailor. When Captain Suckling learned about his nephew's plan he joked: 'What has poor Horatio done, who is so weak, that he should be sent to rough it out at sea?'

Captain Maurice Suckling was the brother of Nelson's mother.

Life at sea

Nelson's father took him as far as London. Then he left the boy to travel alone to Chatham **docks** in Kent. Nelson found his uncle's ship and made his way to a crowded cabin. There he slept in a hammock for the first time.

Learning the ropes

Nelson joined his uncle's ship as a **midshipman**. Midshipmen were junior **officers**, and they could be any age from 12 to 40. They began their training by learning the basic jobs involved in sailing a ship.

As a young midshipman, Nelson climbed the rigging (ropes) to reach the top of the mast where the **look-out** stood. He learned how to put up and take down sails, and he became skilled at raising and lowering the anchor.

Being a sailor in the 1770s was a dangerous and frightening job. Sometimes, look-outs fell to their death from the top of the mast.

A SAILOR'S LIFE

Life on board ship could be very hard – especially for the ordinary sailors. Their day began at 4am and ended after dark. When they weren't busy scrubbing the decks or sailing the ship, sailors had to learn how to fire the guns and fight in battle.

Meals on board ship were very dull. Breakfast was usually porridge. Lunch was dry biscuits and salted meat, and supper was more biscuits and watery soup. Many sailors suffered from **scurvy**, a disease caused by a lack of fruit and vegetables. They developed spots on their legs and their teeth fell out.

It was essential that everyone on board obeyed orders, so discipline was very strict. Disobedient sailors were whipped with a knotted rope called the 'cat-o'-nine-tails'. After this very painful punishment, very few disobeyed again.

This picture shows Nelson (right) as a young midshipman soon after he joined his uncle's ship.

Seeing the world

Once Nelson had mastered the basic skills of sailing, he was keen to go on a long voyage. There was no war, so all the naval ships were staying close to home. Luckily, his uncle found him a place on a **merchant ship.**

Crossing the Atlantic

Nelson's first voyage was to the **West Indies**. As the ship crossed the Atlantic Ocean, Nelson made a discovery – he was terribly seasick! For the rest of his life, Nelson suffered from seasickness whenever there was a storm.

Ice and fever

Just before his fifteenth birthday, Nelson joined a ship heading for the **Arctic**. The aim of the voyage was to find a sailing route around the north of Canada.

VOYAGES OF DISCOVERY

Nelson's voyage to the Arctic was part of an expedition of discovery. In the 18th century, there were many voyages to discover new sailing routes. The most famous explorer was Captain James Cook. He reached Australia in 1770 and also explored the Arctic and **Antarctic** regions.

Nelson was 11 years old when Captain Cook reached Australia. He must have been inspired by the voyages of this great explorer.

Nelson's ship was nearly crushed by icebergs.
He also had a lucky escape from a polar bear.

Nelson's next voyage took him to India. He stayed
in the East for two years, until he caught malaria
(a serious disease that causes very high fevers).
He was so ill that he had to return to Britain. At first
Nelson thought he would die, but on his way home
he had a vision of his shining future in the British
navy. He decided that he had to live.

In the Arctic,
Nelson tried
to fight off a
polar bear
single-handed.
Luckily, a cannon
shot from his
ship scared the
bear away.

Adventures in the Caribbean

When Nelson arrived home from India, he learned that his country was at war. Settlers in America had rebelled against Britain, and had won the support of France and Spain. Nelson decided that he must join the navy and, in spring 1777, he passed the naval exam to be a **lieutenant**.

Taking charge

Nelson sailed for the Caribbean Sea, where the British Navy was trying to prevent any French or Spanish ships from reaching America. He managed to capture several ships and was put in charge of a small warship.

This painting shows Nelson soon after he was made a captain, at the age of 20. In the background is the fort in Nicaragua, which he raided with his men.

At the age of 20, Nelson led a raid on a Spanish fort in Nicaragua, in Central America. He showed great courage, but his men became exhausted and the raid was not a success. Nelson fell ill with **yellow fever** and had to return to Britain to recover.

In 1776, the American Declaration of Independence was signed by all the leaders of the colonies.

Nelson in trouble

Four years later, Nelson returned to the Caribbean. By this time, America was **independent**. Nelson's task was to stop the Americans from **trading** with the **merchants** of the West Indies.

Nelson was so keen on seizing American ships that he upset the local merchants. Some of them even threatened to put him in prison. He had to stay on board his ship for eight months before a court decided to let him go free.

THE AMERICAN REVOLUTION (1775-83)

In the 1700s, Britain owned 13 **colonies** on the east coast of America. The American **colonists** were forced to pay high **taxes** to Britain, which made them very angry. War broke out in 1775 and, on 4 July 1776, the colonies declared their independence. In 1783, the British were defeated and America became an independent nation.

Nelson and Fanny

While he was in the West Indies, Nelson met Frances Nisbett. She was the widow of a doctor and she had a young son, Josiah. Nelson and Fanny were married on the island of Nevis. Soon afterwards, the new family returned to England.

Home – and away

Back in England, Nelson, Fanny and Josiah settled in Norfolk. Nelson's father welcomed them to his home, but it was not a happy time. Fanny hated the cold and Nelson was very bored. He was desperate to return to sea, but Britain was not at war, so no more captains were needed. This all changed, however, in 1792, when France invaded Austria. Britain and Austria were **allies**, so it was clear that war was coming soon.

Frances Nisbett had lived for many years on the tropical island of Nevis. She hated the cold English winters, and wrapped herself up in curtains to keep warm!

In January 1793, Nelson was put in charge of a warship. After five years on shore, he was delighted to be back at sea. In the following month, France declared war on Britain. Nelson sailed towards the Mediterranean Sea and was soon involved in fighting the French.

Injuring an eye

In a battle near the island of Corsica, Nelson was hit in the face by splinters from a bursting cannon ball. His right eye was badly damaged. After that, he was almost completely blind in one eye.

This scene shows an angry crowd coming to arrest the French royal family who had been hiding from them.

THE FRENCH REVOLUTION (1789–99)

In 1789, the people of France rose up in revolt against their king and **nobles**. They seized control of Paris and put the king and queen to death, along with thousands of French nobles. By 1792, a revolutionary army was ruling France. This was the army that **invaded** Austria (see page 14).

Dangerous adventures

In 1797, Nelson played a key role in the Battle of Cape St. Vincent. By this time, Spain was using its powerful navy to support France. The British faced a massive **fleet** of Spanish warships close to the southern tip of Portugal.

Nelson was wounded as he approached the island of Tenerife. His right arm was shattered by a musket ball.

The Battle of the Cape

The British admiral lined up his fleet and gave orders to open fire. Meanwhile, Nelson decided to take some action of his own. Ignoring the heavy gunfire, he sailed straight towards the Spanish ships.

Once on board an enemy ship, Nelson led his men in hand-to hand fighting until the Spanish **surrendered**. Then he boarded a second ship and captured it, too. The battle was a great British victory. As a reward for his bravery, Nelson was made a **rear-admiral**.

Losing an arm

After the Battle of Cape St. Vincent, Nelson continued to fight against the Spanish. One of his battles was fought around the island of Tenerife, which was a base for Spanish troops. Nelson and his men rowed to the island, ready to attack, but just as Nelson stepped ashore he was shot in the arm.

This picture shows the kind of gun, known as a musket, that injured Nelson's arm.

Nelson's bones were completely shattered. He was quickly rowed back to his ship, where a surgeon **amputated** most of his arm.

SHIPS' SURGEONS

Ships' surgeons used knives and saws to amputate arms and legs. There were no **anaesthetics** to put the patient to sleep during an operation. Instead, the surgeons gave their patients a drink of strong rum to help them feel sleepy and to dull the pain.

Fighting Napoleon

Back in England, Nelson waited for his arm to recover. Then he heard the news that the French were planning some new attacks. They had formed a battle fleet under their new commander – the young and energetic Napoleon Bonaparte.

The Battle of the Nile

As soon as he was well enough, Nelson sailed to the Mediterranean to find the French fleet. He guessed that Napoleon would head for Egypt, and try to conquer North Africa. Nelson discovered the French warships in Aboukir Bay, close to the mouth of the River Nile in Egypt.

Just as the light was fading, Nelson ordered his ships to attack. The battle lasted all night, and ended in a British victory. Napoleon's army was left stranded in Egypt.

During the Battle of the Nile, Nelson's head was grazed by gunfire. He had the wound bandaged and quickly came back on deck to continue directing the fighting.

NAPOLEON BONAPARTE

Napoleon Bonaparte rose to power in the years following the French Revolution. As a brilliant general in the French army, he was very popular and, in 1797, he seized control of France.

Napoleon was hungry for power and glory and, in 1804, he made himself Emperor of France. Then he began a campaign to conquer the whole of Europe. By 1812, he had built up a massive empire covering France, Spain and Italy and large parts of Eastern Europe. However, Nelson made sure he never invaded Britain.

Napoleon's downfall began when he tried, and failed, to invade Russia. After this, a powerful group of European countries joined forces against him. Napoleon was finally defeated in 1815, when an army led by the Duke of Wellington won the Battle of Waterloo.

This portrait shows Napoleon when he was the Emperor of France. Napoleon and his forces were a serious threat to Britain.

Nelson and Emma

After the Battle of the Nile, Nelson travelled to Naples in southern Italy. There he was welcomed by Lady Emma Hamilton, who held a grand party for him. Nelson had met Emma five years earlier and they had fallen in love, even though they were both married.

Emma and Horatia

Emma was the lively and attractive wife of Sir William Hamilton, the British ambassador in Naples. After she met Nelson, she followed his adventures closely and the couple wrote passionate letters to each other. Fortunately for Emma and Nelson, Emma's husband was a very tolerant man, and William, Emma and Nelson all travelled back to Britain together.

Lady Emma Hamilton was famous for her beauty and grace.

RESCUING A KING

While Nelson was staying with the Hamiltons, Napoleon's troops threatened to attack the King of Naples. Nelson helped the king to escape to the island of Sicily. The king was so grateful that he gave Nelson the title of Duke of Bronte.

In 1801, Emma gave birth to Nelson's daughter, and they named the baby Horatia. The following year, Nelson bought a house in Merton, Surrey. He lived there with Emma, William and Horatia, after separating from his wife, Fanny.

Turning a blind eye

Soon after his daughter was born, Nelson took part in an attack on a Danish fleet. The Danish ships were anchored in the port of Copenhagen and were defended by guns on shore.

As they started their attack, the British ships faced heavy gunfire. The fleet commander gave the signal to retreat, but Nelson didn't want to give up. He put his telescope to his blind eye and pretended not to see the signal. Then he continued his attack. Later, Nelson was praised for his bold action.

This portrait of Horatia was painted when she was about 14 years old. She is wearing a miniature portrait of her father round her neck.

Preparing for battle

In 1803, Britain declared war on France. Napoleon Bonaparte had been advancing through Europe and now the British feared that they would be invaded. In their time of danger, they turned to their hero, Nelson, to save them.

Hunting the French

The British people hoped that Nelson could find and destroy the French warships. Nelson was made chief commander of the British fleet, and he set off to hunt down the French.

After a long chase, the French took shelter in Cadiz, a port in southern Spain. There they were joined by a Spanish fleet. Nelson decided it was time to attack. On 19 October 1805, he reached the Spanish coast. The enemy ships were waiting for him, just off Cape Trafalgar.

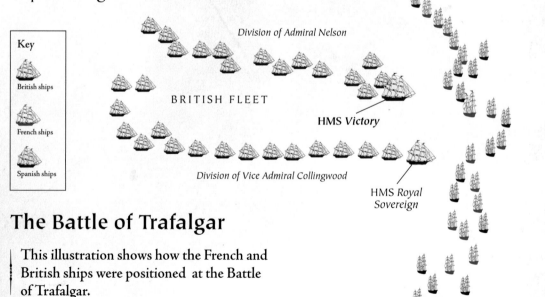

Key

British ships

French ships

Spanish ships

Division of Admiral Nelson

BRITISH FLEET

HMS *Victory*

Division of Vice Admiral Collingwood

HMS *Royal Sovereign*

The Battle of Trafalgar

This illustration shows how the French and British ships were positioned at the Battle of Trafalgar.

HMS *VICTORY*

Nelson's battleship, HMS *Victory*, was built mainly from wood. It had three tall masts, each with a '**crow's nest**' for a look-out. Sailors known as topmen climbed the masts to take in and release the main sails. Others worked on deck, hauling on the ropes.

All the sailors' jobs were hard – especially when the weather was bad. It took a team of around 250 men to turn the capstan (a large winding wheel) that raised the anchor.

Underneath the main deck were the officers' cabins and the crowded spaces where the sailors hung their hammocks. HMS *Victory* also had three gun decks, with a total of 104 cannons. The guns were usually held in place by strong chains, but they were released when battle began.

HMS *Victory* has been preserved at Portsmouth Docks in Hampshire, UK, and is open to visitors.

The Battle of Trafalgar

On the morning of 21 October 1805, Nelson prepared for battle. He positioned his ships between the enemy and the harbour. The British fleet of ships was divided into two columns. Ahead, stretched a line of 33 enemy warships.

'England expects'

Before the battle began, Nelson sent a message to his fleet. The flags spelled out the words, 'England expects that every man will do his duty'.

CHANGE OF MESSAGE

Nelson's famous message before the Battle of Trafalgar could have been different. He gave orders that the message should be, 'England **confides** that every man will do his duty.' The **signalman** asked if he could change 'confides' to 'expects' so that the message would be shorter.

This painting shows Nelson (centre) giving his famous orders to send a message to his fleet.

Fighting began around midday with gunfire on both sides. Many men were injured, and at around 1 o'clock in the afternoon, Nelson was shot by a musket ball. It was clear that he was very badly wounded and he was quickly carried below deck.

Death of a hero

Nelson was in terrible pain, but he still wanted to hear news of the battle. By the afternoon, it was clear that the British had won. Nelson died around 4.30pm, happy that he had saved his country from invasion.

Nelson's body was taken back to London where he was given a hero's funeral. Huge crowds lined the streets to watch the solemn procession to St Paul's Cathedral. Everybody wanted one last sight of an extraordinary British hero.

Why is Horatio Nelson important today?

Nelson saved Britain from invasion. Without his victory at Trafalgar, Britain could have become part of Napoleon's empire. If this had happened, the history of the British people would have been very different. The British might have ended up speaking French!

Nelson and the navy

Nelson was an outstanding naval commander. He was extremely brave and loyal to his country. He was also a great leader in battle, who was not afraid to try out new moves. Today, **naval cadets** still study Nelson's battle plans and are still inspired by his leadership.

This painting by Thomas Davidson is entitled *England's Pride and Glory*. It shows a young naval cadet being shown a portrait of Nelson to inspire him.

The Nelson touch

Above all, Nelson was loved for his kindness to his crew. Everyone who served on his ships felt that he cared for them. He encouraged young sailors when they were frightened, and visited the sick and wounded. After Nelson's death, people began to realise that this personal touch was an important part of a successful navy, and commanders were encouraged to show kindness to their crews.

Through his victories at sea, Nelson made the British navy feared and respected all over the world. Since his time, the leaders of the navy have tried to live up to his example.

After Nelson's victory at Trafalgar, a lasting monument was created for him. Nelson's column was completed in 1843 and stands in the heart of Trafalgar Square in London.

CHURCHILL'S HERO

Sir Winston Churchill was one of many people who have been inspired by Nelson. When Churchill was the British Prime Minister during World War II, he kept a statue of Nelson in his study. He also named his cat Nelson.

A walk through the life of Horatio Nelson

1793

France declares war on Britain. Nelson returns to sea

Nelson's right eye is injured in a battle near Corsica

1794

1789

The French Revolution begins (It lasts until 1799)

Nelson marries Frances Nisbett in the West Indies. Then they return to Britain

1787

1797

Nelson helps to win the Battle of Cape St. Vincent. Later that year, he loses his arm in an attack on Tenerife

1777

Nelson joins the navy and sails to the Caribbean

1775

The American Revolution begins (It lasts until 1783)

1772

Nelson sails to the Arctic

1771

Nelson joins his uncle's boat as a midshipman. Five months later he sails to the West Indies

Nelson is born at Burnham Thorpe, Norfolk

1758

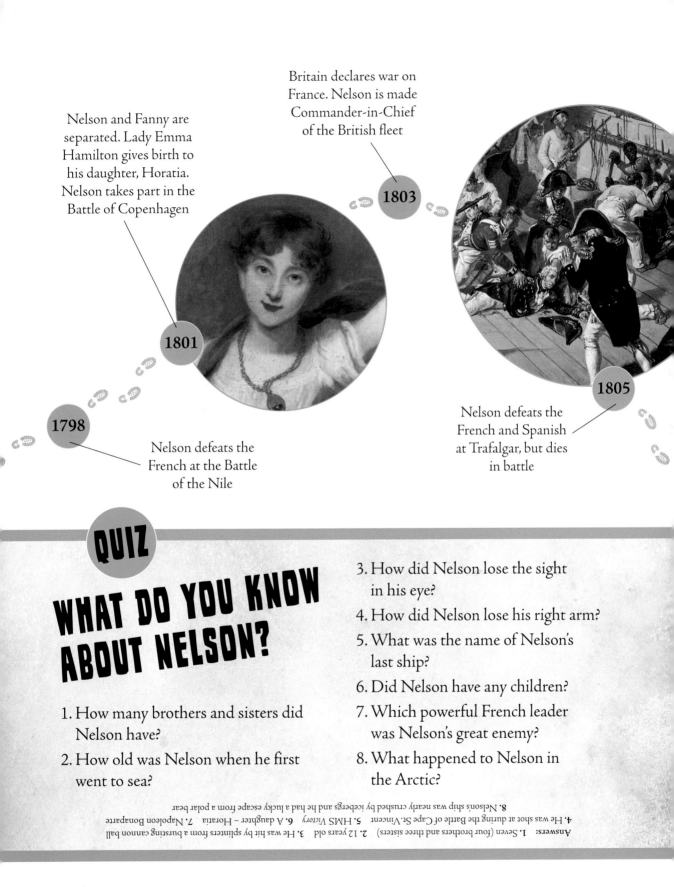

Nelson and Fanny are separated. Lady Emma Hamilton gives birth to his daughter, Horatia. Nelson takes part in the Battle of Copenhagen

Britain declares war on France. Nelson is made Commander-in-Chief of the British fleet

1803

1801

1798

Nelson defeats the French at the Battle of the Nile

1805

Nelson defeats the French and Spanish at Trafalgar, but dies in battle

QUIZ

WHAT DO YOU KNOW ABOUT NELSON?

1. How many brothers and sisters did Nelson have?

2. How old was Nelson when he first went to sea?

3. How did Nelson lose the sight in his eye?

4. How did Nelson lose his right arm?

5. What was the name of Nelson's last ship?

6. Did Nelson have any children?

7. Which powerful French leader was Nelson's great enemy?

8. What happened to Nelson in the Arctic?

Answers: 1. Seven (four brothers and three sisters) **2.** 12 years old **3.** He was hit by splinters from a bursting cannon ball **4.** He was shot at during the Battle of Cape St. Vincent **5.** HMS *Victory* **6.** A daughter – Horatia **7.** Napoleon Bonaparte **8.** Nelson's ship was nearly crushed by icebergs and he had a lucky escape from a polar bear

Cross-curricular links

Use this topic web to explore the life of Horatio Nelson in different areas of your curriculum.

HORATIO NELSON

GEOGRAPHY
Read through the book and make a list of all the places Nelson sailed to. Can you find out where the three main battles that Nelson won took place?

HISTORY
Nelson lived at a very exciting time in history. Why not find out more about:

- The American Revolution
- The French Revolution
- Napoleon Bonaparte

ENGLISH
Imagine that you are a sailor on board HMS *Victory* and write a letter home describing your life on the ship. (The information on pages 9 and 23 will be helpful.)

ICT
During Nelson's lifetime, great voyages of discovery were being made. Look on the Internet to try and find out about the explorer Captain James Cook. The BBC history website is a good place to start.

Glossary

Admiral A naval commander, in charge of a fleet.

allies Friends. Countries become allies to give each other support.

amputated To be cut off.

anaesthetics Drugs or gas given to a patient to prevent them from feeling pain.

Antarctic The frozen area around the South Pole.

Arctic The frozen area around the North Pole.

colonies Countries that are controlled by another country.

colonists People who live in a colony.

confides Meaning 'is confident' or 'trusts'.

crow's nest A look-out platform high up on a ship's mast.

docks An area of water in a port.

fleet A large group of ships.

independent To be free from control by other people.

invaded To be taken over by troops from another country.

lieutenant A junior officer.

look-out Someone whose job is to look out to sea and report on anything new.

merchants People involved in trade.

merchant ship A ship that is used for trade and carries goods.

midshipman Someone who is training to be a naval officer.

navy The ships and sailors that defend a country.

naval cadets Young people who are training to be officers in the navy.

nobles People born into aristocratic or high-ranking families.

officers People who are in charge of other sailors.

rear-admiral A senior naval officer who is two ranks below an admiral.

scurvy A disease caused by a lack of vitamins in the body.

signalman The person in the navy who gave signals to the fleet using flags or lights.

surrendered Gave up.

taxes Money that people have to pay to their ruler or government.

trading The exchange of goods for money or other goods.

vicar A member of the Church of England who looks after people in a parish.

West Indies A group of islands southeast of North America.

yellow fever A virus causing fever and yellowing of the skin.

Index

Numbers in **bold** refer to photographs or illustrations.

Further Information

More books to read

Great Britons: Leaders by Simon Adams
(Franklin Watts, 2007)

*Admiral Nelson: The Sailor who Dared All to
Win* by Sam Llewellyn (Short Books, 2004)

Places to visit

• HMS *Victory*, Portsmouth
• The Nelson Museum, Norfolk
• National Maritime Museum, Greenwich

Useful websites

www.admiralnelson.org
A detailed website about Nelson's life,
with great illustrations.

www.historicdockyard.co.uk/hmsvictory/
Information on Nelson's ship HMS *Victory*.
Includes a video tour of the ship.

www.nmm.ac.uk
The website of the National Maritime
Museum. Type Nelson into the search box to
find information and images about his life,
ships and battles.

Extraordinary Lives

Contents of titles in the series:

WAYLAND